Tasting Moments

Poems by

Pamela Pan

Finishing Line Press
Georgetown, Kentucky

Tasting Moments

ACKNOWLEDGMENTS

Phases, California Writers Club Redwood Anthology, 2023, "Summer Nights."
Center of Attention, Tuleburg Press, 2023, "A Song for a Strong Soul" and "My Home City."
Great Valley Stories, California Writers Club San Joaquin Anthology, 2023, "Farmers Market."

I would like to thank my husband Frank, daughter Amber, and son Darren for their love and support. Without them, I wouldn't be writing poetry.

I'm also grateful to Monique Rardin Richardson for designing the book cover, and Harrie Alley, Cassi Nesmith, Charity Romstad, Rose Cordero-Gonzales, June Gillam, Bill VanPatten, John Britto, Constance Hanstedt, Daniela Fritter, Linda Drattell, Patricia Boyle, Marilyn Dykstra, Monique Rardin-Richardson, Ida Marie Beck, and Ilana Tal for their thoughtful comments and suggestions.

Publisher: Leah Huete de Maines
Editor: Christen Kincaid
Cover Art and Design: Monique Rardin Richardson
Author Photo: Darren Feng

Order online: www.finishinglinepress.com
also available on amazon.com

Author inquiries and mail orders:
Finishing Line Press
PO Box 1626
Georgetown, Kentucky 40324
USA

Contents

The Time Has Come

For you to blow on your stillness.
Rise to the height you're destined for.
Release the "I can't" shackles.

For too long, you've waited,
for opportunities that never come,
saviors who don't save,
superiors who don't approve.

Act now.

The world doesn't pause for self-denial.
If you yearn to travel,
book your ticket.
If you dream of writing a book,
start your first sentence.
Let your critics or inner ego
vent what they will.
Dust off their comments
like cobwebs from your shirt.

The time has come
to shed the shyness of your teenage years,
the ambitions of your twenties,
the exhaustions of your thirties,
the hesitations of your forties.
Now is the time to bloom.

Let the orchestra spring to life,
play the melody you composed—
with you as the main theme and character.

You are the swan on the lake,
the queen and king
of your life.

The time has come.

Stand with Us

Listen.
With the ears of your heart.
Hear us—mothers, sisters, wives, daughters.
The other half of the universe.

We speak in truth,
unlike those who twist words
into weapons and chains,
for self-serving gain.

We are one.
Do not let them divide us.
Those schemers, masters of
pitting men against women,
women against each other,
seek to drag us back into the abyss,
reduce us to servitude—
objects, birthing vessels,
stripped of dignity, robbed of rights.

We've endured thousands of years
of oppression,
clawing up from the abyss,
like the vines of climbing roses,
grasping for handholds on the jagged cliffs,
withstanding battering waves,
resisting relentless winds.

We will not be dragged back.

We are rising.
Our roots and yours,
both deep in this soil
are intertwined, inseparable.
When we flourish, so do you.
The reverse is also true.

Listen
with the ears of your heart.
Stand with us.
Rise.

Grandma's Wisdom

I cook vegetable soup for breakfast,
stirring in chunks of carrot gold,
taro purple, squash green.
Earthy scents waft from the rising steam.
I breathe them in
and think of Grandma.

For her, soup marked the break of the fast.
I still see her widened eyes,
astonished the young couple next door ate
cold rice noodles.
For breakfast? Your body needs warmth—
something with liquid.

For years, I sought wisdom old and new,
on nutrition, on health—
only to return, time and again,
to lessons Grandma taught
before I even turned ten.

Soup for breakfast,
vegetables abundant,
real food for snacks,
and hardest for me, but essential—
follow the natural rhythms,
sleep early, sleep plenty.

Soup ready,
I lift my spoon.
Comfort spreads from tongue to toes.
Grandma's spirit nods.
A perfect way to start the day.

Tasting Moments

Mama set a plate of lotus roots
before my seven-year-old self.
Holes studded the slices like grinning eyes.
Steam rising in soft tendrils.
The aroma wrapped around me
like the sweater of hers I loved to borrow.

I picked up a piece with chopsticks.
"How does it taste?"
Mama's eyes stayed on me.
I chewed,
savoring the crisp crunch and
creamy tenderness.
"Delicious. Can I have another?"
She laughed, turning back to the stove
to prepare the next dish.
I reached for a second piece.

Decades later, at eighty-four,
Mama sits at the table,
watching me sauté
minced pork with tofu.
I set the plate before her,
steam curling up like soft mists.
"Tell me how it tastes."

She scoops up a piece of tofu
drizzled with soy sauce and green onions.
I watch as she takes a bite.
A smile spreads across her face.
"Delicious! I feel so spoiled."
I laugh and return to the stove
to cook the next dish
as she reaches for another piece.

Healing

Mid-autumn full moon floated in the crisp sky,
like a luminous jade palace in Mama's stories.
I traversed an ocean,
reunited with Mama in Tianjin, China.
We savored our dinner of
mackerel dumplings, steamed trout, fresh-baked mooncakes.
Afterward, we strolled to a massage place
to complete the celebration.

The masseuse kneaded Mama's scalp.
Mama groaned.
"Let's spend all eighty-minutes on my head."
"How about tending to full body first," I said.
"Then save extra time for the scalp?"
She'd never had this kind of massage before.
Guilt surged through me as I
melted under the deft fingers of my masseuse.
Had I not left the country,
I would've taken her out more often.

Eighty-minutes zipped past as the young women
pressed and pulled every sinew and joint.
Mama's masseuse dedicated thirty minutes to her head,
focusing on her baihui and fengchi points.
When the session ended,
Mama curled up in the recliner.
"This feels so good!"

Two days later, she asked,
"Shall we go get a massage?"
I laughed and off we went,
becoming regulars,
twice a week, sometimes more.
Our precious afternoons together.
Mama talked more, asking her masseuse
what people ate in her home province of Gansu,
laughed at the description of one long noodle
making up a full bowl.

The front desk scanned my phone for payment—
way more affordable than in California.
But even if it had cost a fortune,
I'd have gladly paid.
Bettering Mama's health,
besides companionship,
topped my goals for the trip.

After a month and a half,
Mama's memory improved,
as did her knee pain.
Eating lunch I prepared,
she held up a hand and closed it into a fist.
"I could only fold halfway before—
and it tingles less."
I wrapped my hand around her proud fist.
My effort and the masseuse's work
had borne fruit.

Under the pale November sky,
I hugged Mama,
my three months sojourn ending.
Brother would take good care of her.
Still, how I wished to bring her
to this side of the Pacific,
even for a few months.
But age, language, health—insurmountable barriers.

December sunlight glided through my window.
My fingers looked slimmer than before.
I'd developed carpal tunnel during the pandemic,
transferring courses online,
typing hours a day for months.
Even when pain subsided
through compresses and stretches,
the swelling remained.
For two years, my wedding ring stayed in a drawer.

Now, from the depth of that drawer,
I retrieved the long-parted ring.
It fit!
In Tianjin, I'd sought Mama's treatment,
But in her healing,
I also healed myself.

Merciless Time

Uncle,
I remember a black-and-white photo of you,
in the living room of Grandma's house.
You stood on the track field,
poised to throw the discus—
right arm swung back, left arm reached forward,
knees slightly bent, chest lifted, eyes forward,
the number 12 bold on your white vest.

You were eighteen, an athletic star,
winning certificates and medals
in national competitions.
Pride and honor to everyone.

If a god of youth existed,
he would look like you,
radiant with vitality,
handsome past description,
strong beyond measure,
like Pan Gu, the deity who pushed up the sky,
allowing light and air to enter.

Uncle, you are the Pan Gu in my universe.
When a bus hit my father's bike and took his life,
leaving Mother a widow,
Brother and me fatherless,
you boarded the earliest train to be by our side.
Mother jumped into the grave the day of the funeral,
wanting to die with Father.
You dragged her back with your discus-trained arms.
"The children need you."

For a year, you journeyed twelve hours each way
to stand by us several times a month,
despite the needs of your own family and career.

We would have floundered,
were it not for you and Grandma.
You secured Mother her first teaching job,
supported her through the most devastating blow.
She could have retreated.
Because of you and Grandma, she overcame,
transformed into a dragon woman.

For Brother and me,
you became a father,
buying our school supplies,
bringing food and clothing.
You made us less like orphans,
more like normal kids,
as normal as fatherless children could feel.

Now, five decades later,
three thousand miles and a Pacific Ocean away,
I listen, helpless,
as Mother and Brother describe your decline.
I cherish the memory of your voice on the phone,
but your hearing had receded.
You kept saying, "I can't hear. I can't hear."
The hearing aid pained you so much
you couldn't use it.
And arthritis in your hands
prevented you from writing.

Multiple strokes stole your agility.
You move slowly, seldom speak.
My powerful, beautiful, strong uncle,
I wish I could hold your hand, talk to you,
find a doctor who would make everything right,
like when I was little, in Grandma's house,
delirious with fever.
In pouring rain, sheltering me in an umbrella,
you pushed me in a cart,

three miles to the hospital.
Water soaked your shirt, pants, and shoes.
But you saved my life.

Age, that merciless corrosive agent of time,
has sunk its teeth into your once-athletic body.
I want to pull those fangs out,
erase your illness, helplessness.
Return you to the beautiful embodiment
of strength and youth in that photo
that is etched in my memory.
Desperation.

Wedding Anniversary

Twenty-nine years ago,
we slid rings onto each other's fingers,
vowing to journey through life together.
And we have,
through sunshine, drizzles, storms.

For this year's anniversary,
we didn't celebrate
with dinner, or a trip to the ocean.
I was in Tahoe for a writing workshop.

"We'll do it next week." We planned
to meet friends in Monterey.
I envisioned us enchanted
by the waves' deep sighs,
as the sun descended
into shimmering water.

The day you were to pick me up,
you texted, "call when you have time."
My heart raced. Sunlight dimmed.
You'd gone to urgent care.
Appendicitis, the doctor said.
Immediate surgery.
Give me a couple days, you replied.
You took antibiotics,
then drove three hours to my side.

I leaned on your chest,
soaking the warmth of the one
who always kept his word.
The next morning, we headed home.
The moment we arrived,
I rushed you to the ER.

I waited in your room
as nurses wheeled you from surgery.
Once so robust and full of energy,
you lay still, eyes closed,
face paler than I'd ever remembered.
I became your protector.

We never made it to the ocean.
Preparing meals for you,
strolling side by side,
talking about feeding the neighbor's cat,
our daughter's San Francisco job,
our son's study abroad in South Korea–
that was enough.

Ahead will be days of light
or nights in storm.
With you by my side,
every moment is a celebration.
May we share countless spans of twenty-nine,
reveling in a union
of true minds
and enduring love.

Half a Century

I'm poised on the sill of a door half closed.
A liminal space.
Time has slipped through my fingers,
like kernels of golden unhusked rice.
I wish I could return them.
All I glimpse is their gleam,
mocking my futile attempts.

The past is half a century old.
But I gleaned nuggets.
As a Chinese saying goes,
once over fifty, clarity rules.
Know when to say "no."
Stand firm to aggressors.
Weigh my own needs as equally as loved ones'.
Prioritize health.
And paramount above all–
spring could still reign supreme.

The door opens to possibility.
I step out,
hear the birds warble,
singing of the season in bloom.

Perhaps I shall dream widely again,
of adventures denied
by the bindings of duty and time.
Now, the yoke falls away.
I step across the sill,
golden grains beckoning.
I revel as they gleam.

Tai Chi

When I say, "I play Tai Chi,"
my friends suggest, "Practice Tai Chi? Do Tai Chi?"
I shake my head.
The heart of Tai Chi is play.
Enjoyment, not chore.
When I part the wild horse's mane,
grasp a sparrow's tail,
stand one-legged like a rooster,
vitality blossoms within me.
I become pure joy,
as Tai Chi intends.

"But how do you play when it's not a game?"
It is a game, though the opponent remains unseen.
Tai Chi is a martial art.
Evey motion involves an invisible partner.
Cloud hands perform a graceful dance,
but it pulls the adversary's hand and strikes back.
White crane spreads its wings strikes an elegant pose,
yet it positions the opponent for an offensive attack.

Tai Chi transforms
self-defense into flowing meditation,
combat into relaxation.
A gamc of joy.
When we play it,
we trot like stallions,
dance like clouds,
soar like cranes,
and merge with the universe.
Energy pours in like light.
Regeneration.

Yin and Yang

We are a goal-setting, goal-getting people
filling our days with tasks,
working long hours,
grabbing meals on the run,
skimping on sleep.

We chase after dreams.
Nothing feels worse
than being still.
Guilt consumes us when we pause,
when we don't produce.

Constant motion leads to chronic exhaustion,
sleep deprivation,
digestive illnesses,
heart disease.

All this striving requires yang—
the golden sun,
the drive to achieve,
the pulse of action.

Yet, yang cannot sustain
if yin is neglected.
The silvery, cooling moon,
the embrace of quiet and rest,
the pause to reflect,
the invisible life force that
rejuvenates body and soul.

Cherish yin,
as we love yang.
There can be no light
without dark.

Summer Nights

Uncle Lu's family built a new house,
with a smooth flat stone rooftop.
On summer days,
they spread out grains of rice,
fresh from the fields,
to dry on bamboo mats.
At night,
after the rice went to sleep in the bins,
as fireflies lit their lanterns and searched for their beds,
we poured water over the roof to cool it,
swept it clean,
rolled out bamboo mats for humans,
lay down to converse with the sky,
vast and endless,
reachable with stretched fingers.

Breeze, the playful guest,
tousled our hair, fluttered our shirts.
Adults talked of land reforms,
someone's betrothal, a cousin's new job.
We the young debated
which teacher was the nicest,
why a man in a movie was so stupid,
whether the blood on his face was real.
We compared the fish we caught,
the rabbits we fed,
the pink deer-shaped sesame cake we ate.

All the while, the smell of new rice drifted into our noses.
The stars gazed into our eyes.
Our voices diminished,
soon murmured into silence.
We drifted into dreams,
while the fireflies flickered on.

Reading out Loud

I fell in love with poetry in seventh grade.
My Chinese teacher wrote a Tang dynasty poem by Li Bai
on a chalkboard.
Four lines, twenty characters,
a clear setting, a sympathetic character,
an unforgettable scene, a rhyming scheme.
It riveted my mind—how could
so few words achieve so much?

For months, I carried a pocketbook
of Tang Dynasty poems,
reading them out loud,
at riverbanks after dinner,
on train rides, during school breaks.

I flipped, twisted, and savored words.
Crunchy like roasted peanuts,
fiery like cayenne,
sweet as watermelons,
hot like dumplings out of a boiling pot.
When I composed, they leaped onto the page.
I became enamored of writing,
following Li Bai's flowing robe.

In graduate school, Boston, 1990s,
I read a paper by an American English teacher
in Qingdao, China.
Influenced by the whole language approach
that emphasized extensive reading,
he lamented how his Chinese students always
read out loud and memorized texts.
They should give up this outdated method, he said,
which dug "a mile deep but an inch wide,"
and embrace the new, scientifically proven way
of language acquisition—silent reading.

He sowed seeds of doubt in my mind,
casting shame over my favorite method.
Had I been wrong in reading out loud?
Did mile deep always lead to inch wide?

Responding to my questions, my professor said,
the article, though well-meaning,
is emblematic of an arrogant American lens,
setting up false dichotomies,
denigrating anything different.
Reading intensely doesn't exclude reading widely.
The Chinese have used the method for thousands of years,
created a marvelous civilization.
Who is this man to say,
all Chinese students must follow the American way?

The professor validated my experience.
Yet, living in America,
I adopted the American way.
Reading miles wide, but seldom out loud.
The harried pace pushed out time for poetry,
let alone those from Tang Dynasty.

Now, as my kids are grown, life slows down,
I finally have leisure to relish again
delicious poems,
and write them too.
That American teacher's opinion, who cares!
Let him whine. Let him wail.
I'm reading poems out loud.
Flip them, twist them, savor them.
Let them pour from my fingers like waterfalls.
Let them nourish my trees whose roots shall extend
a mile deep and a mile wide.

Snow Lotus

Your parents named you Snow Lotus.
Precious flower on the Heavenly Mountain,
snow-white petals defying high altitude,
howling wind,
thin air, thick snow.

Fair skinned like the flower,
eyes gleaming,
quick to laugh and swift to act,
unconcerned about chitchat,
flouting girl conventions,
not wearing dresses,
nor talking quietly.

Your always sweaty palms dampened books.
Your eyes brightened with chemical equilibria,
atomic structure, trigonometric functions.
You groaned over
essays in Chinese
comprehension practices in English.
"Language is not my forte."

We wandered the fields after dinner
at the town's edge
near our high school.
You sang,
soaring from contralto to soprano.
At sixteen, you dreamed of roaming
the endless grasslands of western China,
riding horses into crimson sunsets,
dancing to nomadic flute songs,
sleeping by the Yellow River—
cradle of Chinese civilization.
"That's real life," you said.
You couldn't bear to imagine
a future of unending sameness—
the same job,
the same apartment.

But that was what you got
after college.
A mundane job
in a mundane small town
far from anywhere.
A snow lotus desired for its beauty
and unique qualities.
Your supervisor, a married man,
demanded you be his "Little Third."
Dream lover he called you.

"No," you said. "No!"
Desire twisted into hate.
The company found 12,000 yuan missing,
accused you of embezzling,
ordered you to repay.

Salaried at sixty yuan a month,
you had no money for an attorney or repay.
Your boyfriend left you.
Who wanted to be associated with a potential criminal?
With tear-filled eyes you watched him walk away.
The final pillar of your crumbling life
faded into the night.
You didn't ask him to stay.

A lotus in the snow,
battered by howling wind
frozen to the core.
At twenty-one,
you leapt from the roof of your building.

Now, decades later, I still wish
to ride with you
across western grasslands,
into crimson sunsets,
to reach for the end of the sky.
Snow-white blossom,
eternally blooming.

A Song for a Strong Soul

You hailed from Guizhou Province,
southwestern China,
where high mountains,
capped by stubborn pines, vaporous clouds,
laugh when humans chant, "We shall overcome."
Winding roads reward
the brave, the strong, the respectful
with unforgettable other-worldly sights,
but punish the naive, the foolhardy, the contemptuous.
The weather joins the challenge
with storms, hails, and fog,
testing the mettle of daring souls.

It takes a special kind to live there.
Those who thrive, like you,
embody the essence of the region—
hearty, adventurous, strong.

For your dear daughter
you left the beloved mountains,
landing on the flat lands of Central Valley, California.
Your daughter attended graduate school at night
besides working during the day.
You fed and bathed the grandkids,
took them to school, fetched them home,
cooked your specialty Guizhou dishes—
hot and sour fish, crispy rice with chicken,
buckwheat pancakes stuffed with lamb and ham.

The valley must have seemed strange to you.
The roads straight and flat,
no winding, no cliffs.
Your eyes widened when at 5 a.m.
commuters jammed I-5.
"Don't people sleep? They work too hard."

You missed the perpetual lush green,
the clean mountain air.
But you embraced your new life.
You loved the sun here,
bright and cheery all year long.
Rainy seasons passed fast.
You enjoyed the summers, hot, dry
not humid and stormy, like your hometown.

What didn't you like?
The language.
Mandarin was tricky enough,
on top of the Guizhou dialect you were born into.
Learning to speak English felt like climbing
mountain after mountain.
In your younger years, you might have enjoyed
twisting the tongue like kneading dough.
But not in your sixties or seventies.

You missed your friends in Guizhou,
the parks where you danced every day.
After years of persistence,
you found a group,
Chinese speakers who also loved to dance!
You smiled as if seeing mists melting on peaks,
green and gold.

Your personality stayed the same,
even as you adapted to a new life.
One day in 2021
soon after your seventy-fifth birthday,
on your morning walk,
two men pointed their guns
at you and your husband,
demanding money,

likely thinking two old Asians,
easy targets.
Your husband trembled in fear.

You flung yourself at them,
grabbing their arm, reaching for their gun, shouting in
Chinese,
"Cowards, robbing seniors, *bu yao lian!*"
No face, no dignity, no shame!
The robbers had perhaps never seen
a small Asian woman,
or anyone, so fearless, fierce, furious.
They took off running.
You yelled after them, "Cowards! Bu yao lian! Bu you lian!"
No shame, no shame!

And yet, and yet,
strong and fierce as you were,
cancer took you.
You fought bravely
like you did everything.
In the end, you went up to heaven
your last mountain peak.
I know you are watching from above.
Sunlight brings your laughter.
Dear Auntie,
may the wind carry up this melody,
so you can dance to it.

A song for a strong soul.

Eva

When I think of you,
the word *sparkle* comes to mind.
Your necklaces, rings, bracelets, shoes–
they all sparkled.
And your smile–the brightest.

Your leopard shawl, matching dress, high heels–
you walked like a queen.
When people sought to pigeonhole you–
a Mexican American,
a single woman,
a classified employee serving disadvantaged students,
you tossed a curl of your brown hair,
looked them in the eye.
Your scorching gaze made it clear—
no nonsense.

You grew up in tough communities.
Toughness radiated
from your glistening gowns.
Miscreants steered clear,
when you strode into rough neighborhoods
to convince high school dropouts
about the benefits of college.
Moms brought you water and tamales
when you drove to migrant camps
to show young workers
what education could do for their future.
You cared about the youngsters.
They returned your love
by coming to college,
an alien and intimidating place you made inviting.

You enjoyed chips, beans, enchiladas,
tequila shots.
Your laughed as we sat in El Torito,
talking about classes, students, or whatever.

You threw your head back, hair catching light,
eyes brilliant under layers of eyeshadow,
skin glowing beneath face powder.
Your lips curled upward,
like red crescent moons.

You always did your makeup perfectly–
even in times of sorrow,
like when your parents passed away.
Or when you confronted challenges.
It was your armor,
your readiness to face the world.

Now the most sorrowful time had come, for us.
You lay there, perfectly made up.
Rings shimmered on your folded hands.
Silver threads gleamed on your leopard shawl.
I envisioned you floating to the sky,
waving to us, smiling, your eyes sparkling.
Goodbye,
Eva.

100 Days

I look forward to lunch with my son,
glad he attends college in Sacramento,
close to our home in Stockton.
He'd been feeling fatigued,
with chills and cold sweats.
I pray it's not COVID.

He calls after his checkup with oncologist,
"My leukemia's getting worse.
Doctor says I have 100 days to live."
100 days!
My child.
100 days and his light will disappear?

Oh heaven, how could you be so cruel?
Is this how you repay a mother,
who goes to bed only after
checking her children's homework,
who works and works so they can eat,
who coaches Science Olympia so they can learn,
who takes them to soccer although she'd rather sleep?

And now my child has 100 days.
What am I supposed to do?
Weep for all the sleepless nights I've endured
and the ones to come?
Do I pretend to smile,
tell him to be brave,
make his favorite meals,
plan gatherings with his friends?
Soon they'll be here but he would fade.

Oh my dear son,
I would lay down my life as a bridge.
But how could you cross the rivers inside your body?
I'll be a mountain between you and death.
But my body and soul,

wouldn't be enough to stop
the stealthy steps of the shadow.
Why does heaven choose you instead of me?
Oh why indeed?

My dear child,
perhaps I don't need to do anything more—
I'll simply be with you.
My love stays the same.
Whether you live or not doesn't matter.
I'm with you and always will be.
I can't follow you with my body—it screams to do so!
But my soul will tread by your side,
wherever you go.

Note: I wrote this poem after a friend of mine lost her son, a
child whom I have known since he was a little boy.

The Sorghum and the Earth

A piercing whistle,
an earth-shaking shudder.
The train chugs forward,
parting curtain-thick darkness,
bound for the remote regions of China.

Sorghum stalks flash in headlights,
then recede
into silence and anonymity—
their preferred modes of existence.

Sorghum canes survive the harshest drought,
require little rain or care.
While their siblings—wheat and rice—wither,
sorghum heads raise their brown faces to the sun,
with contented grins.

The passengers on this slow-moving train
are the sorghum of this planet.
Peasants from the vast earth,
their shirts old-fashioned, pants wrinkled,
their Mandarin accented with dialects,
their faces dusted, eyes serene,
their smiles slow, steady.

They'll perhaps never appear in movies or novels.
They live and endure in the backcountry,
unknown, unsung.
Their ancestors weathered the Japanese invasion,
the Civil War, the Great Leap Forward, the Cultural Revolution.
They persevere through locust storms and social upheavals.
Their mantra: survive.

With thin, sinewy shoulders,
calloused, dexterous hands,
weary, resolute backs,
feet firmly planted,
they held up the sky.

Pillars of the world.

Farmer's Market

Hidden under crosstown Freeway 4,
tucked among Washington Street office buildings and stores,
competing with traffic above—
drivers racing for riches don't know what they miss—
a farmer's market, a gem with treasures galore.

Strawberries!
Grapes, apples, mulberries,
freshly picked at dawn,
ripe and juicy, sweet as sunset,
packed with the nutrients your body craves.

Cabbages and cucumbers!
Eat them raw, crunchy and crisp,
taste them cooked, mellow and soft,
add meat or bones,
make a perfect stew or soup.

Peanuts!
Dug before dusk yesterday.
Do you smell the soil?
Wholesome fragrance,
roast or boil.

Tofu!
Firm or soft, your choice.
Low in calories, high in protein.
Have you had tofu puddings?
Delicious with honey or soy sauce.

Eggs, free-range chicken eggs!
Touch the shells, much harder than any stores'.
The yokes, golden yokes, not pale yellow, mind you,
packed with omega-3s, minerals, carotenoids,
delicious in taste, good for immunity.

Salmon, squid, sea-bass!
Wild caught at dawn.
Mother nature's Pacific feast.
Stir-fry them, grill them,
excellent for your heart, fantastic for your nerves.

Come to Stockton.
Search out treasures,
under the overpass.
The market, like the town,
rewards seekers.

Island Trumpets

I climb up the Nounou Mountain,
breathing in scents of resinous pine,
delighting in lava-rich soil,
shy-smile grass,
rain-soaked leaves.

A burst of colors amidst trees.
A rooster on a branch,
ebony and chestnut wings flap,
golden neck feathers shake,
as he opens his crimson bill,
and cries, *Woh-woh-woh-woh!*—
declaring,
what sun, what earth, what life!

Midway down the mountain
a reply flows up,
matching rhythm, matching thrill,
Woh-woh-woh-woh!—

From the summit,
through emerald canopies,
another rooster proclaims,
Woh-woh-woh-woh!—

The mountain echoes
Kauai's trumpet songs,
spreading unfettered joy.

I cast aside my hiking stick,
square my shoulders,
and shout with them.

What sun, what earth,
what life!

Ancient Dwelling

The cave, triangular and small,
measures only three feet at base and height.
Its damp ground hints at recent rain.
I pause—is it worth soiling my clothes to explore?

An elderly lady grunts as she crouches,
her knees refusing to bend.
She lowers herself onto all fours and crawls in.
Reluctantly I follow, inching forward,
ducking under the stone ceiling,
eyes fixed on the light ahead.

Fifty feet in, shoes caked with mud,
I step into wonder.
An enclosed sanctuary—
pines reaching for the sky,
bushes carpeting the ground,
trees ablaze with golden blossoms.

Beyond the yard lies a vast cavern.
Stalactites hang from the ceiling.
Sedimented rocks layer the walls,
witnesses to millions of years.

Early Hawaiian settlers—Polynesian pioneers,
sought refuge in caves.
They preferred those with narrow entrances—
difficult for intruders to breach, easy to defend.
This cave would have been ideal—
its narrow passage deters enemies,
a lush garden offers air, fruit, and space for cultivation,
the cavern provides ample room for living.
Settlers must have made it their home.

I've hesitated to enter, but now I dread leaving
this ancient dwelling with untold history.
How did its inhabitants survive?

What secrets lie etched in these stones?
I yearn to know, but silence is the only reply.
The cave guards its secrets.
A vault of time.

Oahu Grounding

The ocean's hues shift
from clear to emerald,
then to deep indigo,
until the water embraces the sky,
in a brilliant azure.

Pale, soft sand,
rises to envelop my toes,
tickling and soothing.
Waves roll in, caress,
drawing sand and stress away
with their retreat.
Fresh energy flows in.

Perfect grounding.

Pamela Pan is an English professor at San Joaquin Delta College, where she teaches and does research on reading, writing, and literature. She has a PhD in Education from the University California, Davis, a Master's degree in Bilingual/ESL Studies from the University of Massachusetts, Boston, and a Bachelor's degree in Engineering from Shanghai Jiao Tong University in China.

Pamela is a writer of poetry, essays, and fiction. She has received a fellowship and attended the Community of Writers' summer writing workshop. Her story "Baba's Accordion" was published in California Writers Club's *Best of the Best: 2024 Literary Review*. Her work has appeared in various magazines and anthologies, including *Poets' Espresso Review, Center of Attention, Phases, Great Valley Stories, Voices of the Valley,* and *Vision and Verse 2024*. Her article "Turning Family History into a Historical Novel" is featured on the Historical Novel Society North America website.

In her spare time, Pamela enjoys walking, listening to audiobooks, and spending time with her family.

Pamela Pan's social media links:
Facebook: https://www.facebook.com/home.php
X: https://x.com/Pamelalpan
Instagram: https://www.instagram.com/pamelapanwriter
Bluesky: https://bsky.app/profile/pamelapan.bsky.social
LinkedIn: https://www.linkedin.com/in/pamela-pan-ph-d-11223 549/